Married
BY MYSELF

LIVING A PARALLEL LIFE WITH A MAN HIDING BEHIND THE CLOTH

LAURIE SULLIVAN

Published by Victorious You Press™
Charlotte NC, USA

TITLE: MARRIED BY MYSELF

First Printed: 2023

Cover Designer: Jadia Sullivan

Editor: Amanda Smith

ISBN: 978-1-959719-07-6

ISBN: (Ebook) 978-1-959719-08-3

Library of Congress Control Number: 2023906152

Printed in the United States of America

For details email joan@victoriousyoupress.com

or visit us at www.victoriousyoupress.com

Dedication

To God, first and most of all

"Now unto Him who is able to keep you from falling, and to present you faultless before the presence of his glory with exceeding joy, to the only wise God our Savior, be glory and majesty, dominion, and power, both now and ever. Amen." Jude 1:24-25 (KJV)

To my sons, all valiant men of God

To my Rob, there are no words . . .

To all the women who did the journey with me

To my readers who have known deception . . . may you also know He who brings life to your bones!

Foreword

I have known Laurie for over 50 years, and I am thankful she has the courage to share her life's journey. Her courage, strength, trust, and joy in the Lord is evident all through her journey. This testimony is of how God was with her each step she took, each place she worked, and the beautiful boys who all grew in strength by God's grace.

One common denominator among people who have journeyed a similar path, felt alone and oftentimes manipulated is that the truth about their personal value and worth is broken. My husband and I have personally wept with people we have grown to know over the years and who have walked similar paths. The one truth anyone can hold on to is the love of the Father. This book can bring encouragement in dark times for anyone who is married by herself.

Danita Drost Burks

Pastor's wife: 35 years

Mother of three boys

Clerk of Courts, Floyd County Indiana

Table of Content

Introduction

Dear Reader,

Got pain?

Me, too.

The greater question is . . .

Got, God?

Yes? Good. You're going to need Him because this whole gig is done East of Eden.

My Cinderella dreaming naïve self, married not only a handsome prince, but one who seemed to love my Jesus just as I did. After all, he was a Bible school junior who was studying youth ministry which was a perfect fit for my future career as a high school English teacher.

Except he didn't . . .

love Jesus or me.

He tortured my mind through **gaslighting**, repeated affairs, and pornography. He crushed my self-esteem and left me so broken after nine years.

The best news is I met Jesus Christ long before I knew my husband's name, and Jesus was not a religion to me, but my personal Savior, refuge, counselor, and strength. And that is why I live victoriously, East of Eden.

This is my story, but it's actually for you. In the throes of suffering (the kind that features the "ugly cry"), I begged God to let me use my pain someday to help someone else.

Each chapter begins with a song and a statement of faith. Please search each Turn it UP reference on your favorite music streaming platform or the internet. Listen to the words that God has always used to reach my beleaguered soul. The "I Believe" section represents the infallible words of truth that lived long before I did and will remain long after I am dancing with Jesus!

"I've Got Confidence"

recorded by Andre Crouch and the Disciples

I Believe

"... but there is a friend who sticks closer than a brother."

Prov. 18:24 (AMP)

Chapter One

Bottom line. I was married to a pedophile, a sexual predator, and a porn addict. To make it all more bizarre, he was a youth minister. I wish I could say there was a moment when I clearly understood the facts and acted promptly; however, there were many moments of suspicion. Gray areas as you will. Moments when I thought I saw "A," but he explained it away. Created enough doubt that I questioned my own sanity. I know what that is now: **gaslighting**. I lived in it for nine-and-a-half years and thankfully, I got out with my marbles intact. I attribute that to a real God. I have called Jesus Christ my Savior and Refuge since I was four years old and have learned to ask Him about everything and wait for His guidance. And sometimes that wait can seem like an eternity.

My clarity came in such an odd way. It was a Friday night and dinner was finished. Doug had left for the office about 30 miles away. After being fired from our last pastorate, he became a professional counselor who "counseled" people. Doug worked at night while I taught high school during the day. Our boys were eight, six, and three and were in school and daycare. The boys were playing in the back yard where I could see them clearly from the window at the sink where I was washing the dishes. As usual, our life situation weighed heavily on my mind. Another week had gone by, and insanity had become routine.

We were in month seven of living in a rental house in the city where Doug had been fired as senior pastor after several "sightings" of him in compromising situations with a 17-year-old high school girl who was in my Sunday school class. Since more than one board member had seen him and questioned his choices, they finally decided to fire him. The **gaslighting** bit that came from this was Doug telling me the board members hated "ME". I cried in shock because I loved those people. We built our congregation from 12 to 130 in the few years we had worked there. I loved the Friday nights in the park with music, the Wednesday night Ephesians study

I taught while Doug met with the youth group downstairs, the preschool I started, VBS, the nursery staff, and our worship team. Doug told me NOT to contact any of the people from the congregation.

He said to me, "Laurie, you think those people love you. They don't. They HATE you."

"They fired me for leaving the lights on in the building while we were on vacation. They fired me and hired the guy who preached for us when we were gone!"

Sounds crazy, I know. Did I believe it? Partly. But the **gaslighting** had been going on for nine years, and I was broken. I didn't even dare to drive the car more than six miles to work and back. Me! Educated me. Godly childhood me. No Bachelor of Science degree can protect a person from **gaslighting**. No godly parents or loving family can protect a person from **gaslighting**. Thus, our family moved out of the parsonage to a rental property. Daily, the older boys and I went off to school after dropping little Josh at the sitter's house. Doug left for his office in the city usually before we came home, so we saw him infrequently. I prayed. I prayed. I prayed, and I worked. I cared for my precious boys moving through all of life in some stupefied fog waiting on God to give me solid direction on WHAT TO DO.

Doug did crazy things. On Saturdays, he would pass out on the couch leaving a sleeve of Benadryl meds on the coffee table, so I could see just how many Benadryl he had consumed. He laid drooling on the couch while the boys tried to wake him to play with them. On another occasion, he came into the living room with a pack of Marlboro cigarettes showing through his shirt pocket. I could sense the confusion from my boys through their eyes, so I tried to get Doug out of sight as soon as possible…before the questions began.

But that night while I was washing dishes, God dropped two words in my mind: tough love. I felt these two words so strongly that I stopped moving my hands in the water. "Tough love," I thought. I had heard this somewhere before.

"I bet the Christian bookstore in town would know. There must be a book about that!" I dried my hands and left the rest of the dishes in the sink because the bookstore closed at 6:00 p.m. and it was 5:40. It was like

I had been supernaturally drawn to the car. I called for the boys to pile in.

"Do you have a book called tough love? I immediately asked the clerk.

"No," she said, "but there is a book called *Love Must Be Tough*."

"I'll take that."

After I got the boys down for the night, I had read half of the book and by Saturday morning, I had finished it. The book encourages women to set boundaries for themselves, and suggested I write a letter, so I did, to Doug. I called our former youth pastor and his wife to come witness me giving Doug the letter. The letter told him to leave the house. As I headed to the grocery store to make copies of the letter as proof of the original in case Doug tried to destroy it, I was violently shaking.

There was another moment of clarity that confirmed my decision to tell Doug to leave. The guiding hand of my Savior. That morning Doug's briefcase was in the car; he never left it in the car, but in that briefcase was my objective proof, my evidence for the man who had been **gaslighting** me for years. I remember standing there in the parking lot. When I opened the briefcase, I found the evidence I needed…the office telephone bill from last month. There were calls to two women whose numbers I knew. There were 33 calls to Angela at different times and 17 calls to MacKenzie. For the first time, I had evidence in my hand that Doug could NOT explain away. He was having multiple affairs using his counseling office in the city as a base to find his victims.

As I drove home with my heart beating firmly and uncomfortably, I thanked God aloud for giving me resolve, for the book He guided me to purchase, for the unexpected find of the phone bill, for Jessie and Trent who were meeting me at the house, and for blessed clarity.

God had led me to this moment. Within my body I was consumed with fear. My palms were sweaty, and I could feel lumps in my throat. I felt firm resolve rooted in full confidence that my faithful God was leading. I beat Jessie and Trent to the house. As I entered the home, I tried to act normal. It was odd for me to travel anywhere by myself, so Doug was questioning me. I think the boys were napping at this time; I honestly can't remember, but I do know I would not have been able to rest if the boys weren't safe. Suddenly, the doorbell rang. As I went to open the door, I said, "Oh, I invited Jessie and Trent over."

Once they were seated, I read the letter aloud to Doug. I didn't give him the chance to say much to them. With the letter and a copy of the phone bill in hand I found in Doug's car, there was nothing Doug could say. He was silent for a while before admitting the truth; claiming the affairs were "emotional affairs" as he had always done.

"I guess I gave my life to God but never my heart," he said.

"Well, let's do that now, my brother," Trent offered.

Silence.

Silence, the deafening silence.

Doug studied the carpet.

It took a month and the anticipated arrival of my parents coming to town for a visit, to spur him out the door. He claimed he didn't have the money to leave me right away (let's savor that statement for a moment), but the Friday before my parents arrived from out-of-state, he was gone. And with him, left all my dreams of marriage, parenting, and growing old with someone I adored. All of it. Gone. It would be a while before I realized that for most of the years of our marriage, I had been married by myself.

gaslighting: *noun*   The Merriam-Webster's 2022 word of the year.

1. Psychological manipulation of a person usually over an extended period of time that causes the victim to question the validity of their own thoughts, perception of reality, or memories and typically leads to confusion, loss of confidence and self-esteem, uncertainty of one's emotional of mental stability, and a dependency on the perpetrator

2. The act or practice of grossly misleading someone especially for one's own advantage

gaslighting: *verb (used with object)*

to cause (a person) to doubt his or her sanity through the use of psychological manipulation:

(dictionary.com)

Turn It Up

"All the Way My Savior Leads Me"

written by Fanny Crosby in 1875

recorded by Chris Tomlin

I Believe

"The Lord is my Shepherd [to feed, guide, and shield me], I shall not lack. He makes me lie down in [fresh, tender] green pastures; He leads me beside the still and restful waters. He refreshes and restores my life (myself); He leads me in the paths of righteousness [uprightness and right standing with Him – not for my earning it, but] for His name's sake. Yes, though I walk through the [deep, sunless] valley of the shadow of death, I will fear or dread no evil, for You are with me; Your rod [to] and Your staff [to guide], they comfort me. You prepare a table before me I the presence of my enemies. You anoint my head with oil;

my [brimming] cup runs over. Surely or only goodness, mercy and unfailing love shall follow me all the days of my life, and through the length of my days the house of the Lord [and His presence] shall be my dwelling place." Ps. 23:1-6 (AMP)

Chapter Two

I wanted to be married. My parents, Barry and Mae were married. I had two sets of grandparents who were also married. All sixteen sets of my aunts and uncles were married. It was like marriage ran in my family. Realistically, I knew marriage was work. My parents were models for me. Neither of them was perfect, but they loved each other . . . in my face. . . all my life. When I spoke at my daddy's funeral, I jokingly stated, "I could not have been married to Barry; it would have set me crazy." I also said, "I could not have been married to Mae either; I would have ended up in the funny farm." But they loved each other. . . and Jesus. . . and me. So, I wanted that journey, too. Marriage sounded good, especially in Ephesians 5:

"Wives be subject to your husbands (OK, that could be tough all by itself but read on) . . . husbands love your wives as Christ loved the church and gave Himself up for her." Eph. 5:25 (AMP)

A guy who would love me enough to die for me?

Sign Me Up.

Marriage would provide me with a forever person.

My person. My very own person . . . ahhhhhhh.

Partner in adventures . . . someone to grow old with . . . to hold hands with when I'm 90. I was all about that. I still am.

Ironically enough though, I was married by myself. Oh, he was there live . . . in person, but I was alone. Alone in gradually every way a person can be alone. Alone with son number one, son number two, and son number three. (Well, clearly, I was NOT alone on at least 3 occasions.) And if the loneliness was not dreadful enough . . . there was more. We were in ministry; he was a minister.

When a person is facing divorce from a minister, she loses a lot so quickly.

In the moment of his decision that he...

Doesn't love you

Found someone else

Wants out

Is tired of it

Never loved you

And/or any other characteristic vernacular from the Prince of DARKness . . .

In just a single moment she has lost . . .

her pulpit presence,

her spot on the worship team,

her Bible Study teaching on Wednesday nights . . .

And yet, there is more. . . if church was her only job, she just lost that and her house. The parsonage is for the paid personnel. Her money is gone, and so is the house.

And . . . she has lost her social circle. Parishioners shy away from her unable to articulate their feelings for her, lost in their own despairing thoughts: "If the man of God is lost, what hope is there for me?" As well, fellow men-of-the-cloth and their wives stay busy with their congregations, too, as if the devastation is contagious.

Look this pain square in the face:

No ministry

No job

No house

No friends

No husband

No happily-ever-after- 'til-death-do-us-part

That was now my reality. Doug was off to pursue his life and just when I was spinning numb with the depth of understanding that cripples and paralyzes, God spoke:

"Mommy, we need cereal." (Well, that's how he spoke to *me*. Jesus Christ who had known me from birth knew exactly how to speak to me in that moment.)

My three chocolate-eyed little boys all bare feet and wearing pajamas . . . NEEDED. There were days following the separation when the divine reason that I pulled my robotic carcass up out of bed to face another day. My three boys needed to eat cereal. Period.

The first night I tucked those boys into bed, I was alone, and now in every way a person could be alone. I walked down the stairs of the house we were renting, into the darkness of that spring night. A myriad of lights peeped softly through my living room window from the outside. I was drawn to stand there in the silence.

Very quietly, I said, "God, can we really do this? You and me?"

I was so afraid of loneliness, of my own uncertainty, of the mammoth financial responsibility. I was afraid I wouldn't know how to raise three boys. I only had one brother, and every time my mother came to visit, she always reminded me that raising boys was so different, so loud and so physical.

"Do they have to *touch* each other every time they pass by each other?"

Push. Shove. Bang. Thud. And, then there were the terms of endearment: butthole, fat, stupid, etc.

The thought came into my mind...what if I did something wrong, unknowingly? What if what I do messes them up so badly that they end up on some TV talk show? I look back on that night now and smile. What a journey it has been since then. Ice hockey practice. Snowstorm trips to games. All the bench-mom moments for football, baseball, basketball, swimming, and soccer. We did homework, acted in musicals, joined a church, took summer vacations. We bought corsages. Rented tuxedoes. Learned how to drive . . . even a manual transmission, eh? But most of all, we prayed. We all prayed to our God for absolutely everything. Turns out God knew how to raise a boy; I just needed to be the mom, the praying mom.

This is a story told from "the other side" of pain. Over here, where it is now safe. Where I can assure you as I walk through the memories and their sordid details there IS hope. . . not only from this side, but . . .

all
along
the
way.

"Live for Jesus"

recorded by Evie Tournquist

I Believe

"For God so loved the world,

That He gave His ONLY begotten son

That whosoever believes in Him

Should not perish but have everlasting life."

John 3:16 (KJV)

Chapter Three

It's been so long. So long I have been in love with Jesus.

I was four.

I know.

Four, Laurie? What did you even know? What could you even know about spiritual matters at that age? Fair enough, but I confessed my "sin" of stealing rhubarb from the neighbor's garden . . . rhubarb, I know . . . no candy or fudge for me! However, it was wrong and even my four-year-old self knew it, so when I knelt to pray and ask Jesus to come into my heart, forgive me of my sins, and let me live in heaven with Him someday, I felt good.

The rest is history as they say. I grew up with Jesus. I loved Him a lot. . . in my childish way. The more I learned about Him, the more peace I found.

I prayed a lot…at breakfast, lunch, and dinner and before I went to bed. As I grew older, I would stare out the car window…watching as Maine's highways and back roads rolled by and just talked to God. I mean when you live in Maine and your dad is a minister, you spend a lot of time in the car. There was nothing unnatural about me looking in the sky and talking to Jesus as the pine trees disappeared in the rearview as our car passed by. My prayers weren't formal; they were conversations between a girl and her God.

By the time I was 12 years old, I had read the entire Bible as part of the curriculum for our church's Honor Star program. Of course, at that age there was a lot I did not fully understand. However, from what I learned, I knew I could trust God, and when I turned 13, I had a chance to put it to the test. The 'ole rubber was about to hit the road.

While God was my first love, my second came strolling through the back door of the sanctuary on a

Sunday night while I was getting my tambourine tuned for some gospel singing. He had on a navy three-piece brushed cotton suit accessorized with a confident smile. His light brown hair was shoulder length and blew back gently in the breeze as he walked forward. All 14 of us girls…yep 14…stopped. We all just froze with the look of stupidity, I'm sure, as Jenna calmly stated, "that's my cousin, Andrew, home from Sweden now."

After only four months as Andrew's gal, my father decided he would minister at a church 536 miles away. At age 13, my only recourse was to scurry to my bedroom and grieve. This was awful. Unfair. I was leaving Andrew; the guy who saw me and had found value in me. He chose me out of a group of 14 other girls. He was just two years older than I, but he had lived as a missionary's kid in Sweden. He was somewhat mysterious and exciting, not to mention cute. Yikes! He loved Jesus like me. We talked and talked. And kissed. Ah, those kisses! "Jag alskar dig" (I love you in Swedish) was what he wrote in the front of my Bible. Andrew's love for me changed how I viewed myself, forever!

I wept alone in my bedroom when daddy announced that we would leave. And I mean wept with guttural noises and lots of snot; I was powerless. After the weeping subsided enough for me to see my Bible, I grabbed it and opened it randomly. Missionaries and evangelists had spoken for years about God meeting them in desperate moments by simply opening their Bibles.

"Follow me" was the italicized header on the top of the page. I froze. John 21 was the chapter where Jesus had asked Simon Peter if he loved him three times.

"After breakfast Jesus said to Simon Peter, 'Simon, son of John, do you love me more than these others?'

'Yes,' Peter replied, 'you know I am your friend.'

'Then feed my Lambs,' Jesus told him.

Jesus repeated the question: 'Simon, son of John, do you really love me?'

'Yes, Lord,' Peter said, 'you know I am your friend.'

'Then take care of my sheep,' Jesus said. Once more he asked him, 'Simon, son of John, are you even my friend?'

Peter was grieved at the way Jesus asked the question this third time. 'Lord, you know my heart; you know I am,' he said.

Jesus said, "Then feed my little sheep.'

. . . Then Jesus said, Follow me.

Peter turned around and saw the disciple Jesus loved following, the one who had leaned around at supper that time to ask Jesus, 'Master, which of us will betray you?' Peter asked Jesus, 'What about him, Lord? What sort of death will he die?'

Jesus replied, 'If I want him to live until I return, what is that to you? **You follow me.**'"

(John 21:5-22 *The Living Bible*)

I was frozen. Quieted. Breathing normally. God had spoken: "Follow me." I have never forgotten the encounter, the moment that Divinity spoke to a broken child. Never.

I had a very lonely teen life where I was living out west. Never would I ever know the bountiful joy of a pile of friends like I had back East. My friendship with Bobbi got me through those lonely years. Sure, I knew a lot of people, but the connections were never the same. I met Doug when we first moved there. His dad was the music leader and choir director. Doug played the trumpet in the orchestra, so he was present every Sunday. Doug was a nice-looking guy with dark brown hair and a decent height for a girl who stood at five feet three inches tall. His German-Italian skin tanned without effort, but he was arrogant and cocky. I was not attracted to him at all. Bobbi became his on and off again girlfriend for three years. I witnessed him cheating on her at camp one summer and was sick to my stomach. Once when we were 17, I took Bobbi's face in my hands and said, "Bobbi, just break up with him; he's such a jerk." I had grown weary with having to listen to her cry about his last infraction; I mean it had been three YEARS!

When I was 15-years-old, Doug and I had a bitter experience. During a youth group sponsored Rock-a-

Thon, Doug had spiked the punchbowl and kept insisting I drink from it. Stupid.

"Just leave me alone. Do whatever you want to do but leave me out of it. You're never interested in me or what I do, so why are you nagging at me to drink your stupid punch?" I said to Doug.

That saga ended with me calling my dad who was our minister, at 2:30 a.m. to shut Doug up. The fallout ended with Doug and his wine buddies leaving with their parents around 3:00 a.m.; I was the most hated person in the because all three perpetrators lied and said I was just making it up. Glorious! I endured two weeks of church services from hell …. oxymoron, eh?

Church, at that time, meant attending two services on Sunday, youth group, and bible study on Wednesday nights. Each moment in the house of the Lord where the stares and whispers were loud enough to send any young Christian flying out the door, never to return. And to make matters worse for me, Doug's oldest brother was the speaker one Sunday night. He was home from Bible college, and to encourage aspiring preachers, my dad would give them time in the pulpit. Greg gave a whole sermon about the dangers of a lying tongue and how God hates that.

Thanks, Greg!

I wanted to flee the building, but my mother wouldn't let me, "You hold your head up high like the princess you are," she said. As she opened her Bible to quietly read scripture, I listened only to the sound of her voice. I made it through that church service.

Then, it came…the mercy of God. One night, the mom and the teenage girl from the Rock-a-Thon came to the door. Next, a dad and the teenage boy from the Rock-a-Thon, and then, Doug's dad. They ALL confessed. I was finally cleared from being a "liar," but not before some hefty damage had been done to my heart. At one point, Doug's mom had even cornered me at the water fountain in the church foyer. She called me a liar and proclaimed that I would never be invited to youth group parties at her house, all while pointing her finger in my face and practically screaming. Saved by my youth pastor, I was whisked down the steps and out the door. I shook, and I cried.

Stupid Doug. Stupid "Christian people". How 'bout ANYBODY acts like Christ?

"Stand in Faith"

recorded by Danny Gokey

I Believe

"Go then and make disciples of all the nations, baptizing them into the name of the Father and of the Son and of the Holy Spirit. Teaching them to observe everything that I have commanded you, and behold, I am with you all the days (perpetually, uniformly, and on every occasion) to the (very) close and consummation of the age. Amen (so let it be)

Matt. 28:19-20 (AMP)

Chapter Four

When I was 19 . . . yes, 19 . . . I married him. It was the summer between our sophomore and junior year of college. I know . . . I know.

In my defense . . .

Well, there is really no defense. I was naïve, an optimist, and a fierce fighter for the underdog and justice. There was a time in 6th grade when I got sent to the principal's office for defending my timid and sweet friend, Kim. Our booger-flinging math teacher demanded Kim take off her "coat." First of all, it was NOT a coat, it was a jacket that matched her pantsuit. It was very stylish and trendy in the 70's. Secondly, when she meekly answered that her mom had purchased the outfit for her, he roared at her again…telling her to take it off. I stood.

Yep. Stood. The minister's daughter who knew the commands of God and who had been taught by her parents…obedience and respect for elders. We both were sent to the principal's office. No penalties for either of us. What on earth was booger-flinger thinking? But that was always me, the empath. So, when Doug arrived at college to become a youth minister, I observed his growth and how he had changed from his incessant conceit in high school. I had now seen his heart for Christ and for working with teenagers. I had fallen into the classic girl belief, the one that too many movies and books portray. With me as his partner, my heart could encourage his heart toward goodness. Sigh. Free will, you know?

I married him. Married him against my parents' advice and wishes. Married him against his mom's wishes. His mother had told my mom that she was doing everything she could to stop the wedding and expected that my mom would do the same. So, marital bliss, it was!!

Honestly, it was funny when Doug first called my dorm room. He was attending a different college in town. He called to ask MY advice on how to get girls at his school to date him. I guess all his former strategies were no longer working for him. *Bahaha.* All I could say was, "Well, Doug, welcome to the world where the rest of us live." I agreed to let him come roller skating (don't laugh . . .that was the gig in college . . . really) with me and my friends on Friday nights. Looking back on things, I now wonder if it was the fact I knew the city, had been there first, and was established and living on my own...that provided him with a challenge. What caused him to become interested in me after Sonya, Julia, and Rachael had all turned him down? I didn't need him. I didn't want him. I felt sorry for him. But he asked me out that May and acted like a perfect gentleman. Impressive. We dated about eight months before he proposed. I accepted his proposal, but it didn't last.

Once, after he had broken off our engagement, he called to talk to me. I listened to him cry. I knew I was going to be OK because of the counseling I put myself in and even though I was looking forward to my future without him…hearing him cry shook me. He said all the repentant words people say after they've cheated and have realized what they lost or were about to lose. I distinctly remember getting out of his red car in the rain, shutting the door with one last glance at him:

This is the moment.

This is the crossroad.

I am in it right now.

What I do here will determine forever.

I forgave him. I forgave him for breaking my heart completely and carelessly, breaking off the engagement, sending his friend to pick up my beautiful diamond ring, and for tarnishing every dream I had about working for Jesus as a team. Like Mary in *It's a Wonderful Life*, I dreamt of working alongside a good man. She had married George Bailey, a good man and was working alongside him at the Building and Loan, celebrating young couples as they purchased their first home…joyously.

So, with that in my heart, I forgave him. I forgave him again even after he deliberately sat in MY dormitory lounge laughing with his new chick, Heidi. Essentially, I had already forgiven him when I cried in agony to God weeks before. I forgave him because that's what Christ would want. I forgave him because Jesus was my first love, and I would always be safe and adored by Christ. I forgave him during my counseling sessions. Thus, we would move forward as a power couple for Jesus. He would become a youth pastor. I would become a high school English teacher. We would work with teenagers and love them to Christ. Together!

When we were split-up, I went on a date with my R.A., Dottie's brother, Jeff, who had seen me in her suite when he was fixing her stereo. Feeling a bit nervous and scared, I was also soothed and flattered...flattered that Jeff wanted to meet me because there were at least seven other girls in Dottie's suite that day. We went to a football game and out for some Springfield, Missouri style cashew chicken. I enjoyed his intelligence and sense of humor, so when he asked me out on a second date to watch one-act plays at the local university, I said

"Yes." We shared an interest in theater and that was energizing and fun! But, after Doug called and sobbed his heart out to me about his wrong choices, begging me to consider a great future we would have working for Jesus together (you know, the 'ole Satan-had-derailed-him story), I told Jeff I could not go on a second date. I was honest with him and said, "Doug called me and wants to try again."

"This is a relationship that may last forever, and I need to try," I declared.

He simply replied, "What if we are a relationship that could last forever, Laurie?"

What if?

Our marriage counseling was pitiful. Doug's older brother was going to perform the ceremony, so he counseled us. And I really don't remember much, except that Greg was a funny guy, and that I laughed a lot.

My parents, God bless them, conducted themselves gracefully. I asked my father to not be part of the ceremony; I just wanted him to be my dad that day. He walked me down the aisle with dignity, prayer, and hope. I assured them both that Doug had changed; he really was humbled during college and wanted to be in ministry just like they were! They were honorable people who lived with integrity.

So, in May following my sophomore year in college, Doug and I drove home to be married, had no honeymoon because we both had minimum wage jobs waiting for us that summer…and two more years left of college. We were young, giddy, and fearless with a solid future ahead of us. To add to our joy, Doug's other brother, Jeb and his new wife, Lindsey were coming to college with us. We had gotten them the apartment next door to us in a brand-new apartment complex near Doug's college campus. It was summer in the Midwest, warm and humid with perfect air-conditioning running in the house. I was married to this handsome, "full of crap" jokester who could cry in front of a woman and pray like he knew God intimately. We made it!

"Go Light Your World"

recorded by Kathy Trocolli

I Believe

"You, however, are not in the realm of the flesh but are in the realm of the Spirit, if the Spirit of God lives in you."

Rom. 8:9 (NIV)

"No test or temptation that comes your way is beyond the course of what others have had to face. All you need to remember is that God will never let you down; he'll never let you be pushed past your limit; he'll always be there to help you come through it."

I Cor. 10:13 (MSG)

Chapter Five

We didn't make it one year before the pornography. I found it in his briefcase, the one we purchased with the combination lock for his overall professional appearance. The glossy pages of various magazines were hanging out of his briefcase enough for me to notice that something was amiss. As naïve as I was, I knew *Oui* didn't mean, "oui" (high school French major). Because of the combination lock, I couldn't open it. I had to wait to ask Doug about it. Pregnant with our first child, 20-years-old and a junior at a Christian liberal arts college, I was nauseated and afraid of the confrontation. Doug calmly explained he had been counseling a 15-year-old guy in our small church youth group who had given the stash to him in an act of repentance; Doug just hadn't trashed it yet.

I bought that.

Not really, but I wanted to, you know. I needed to.

We made it through two years of marriage as college students and new parents. I never again found evidence of the pornography, and we seemed to be past it. Our beautiful baby boy was born two weeks before my senior year began, and life was full of changes and responsibilities. Chad Douglas weighed in at seven pounds, two ounces. He had this perfect little man head. Really. I had envisioned having a Gerber baby and he was more . . . Al Pacino. I could comb his hair into a side part, and he had no baby chub cheeks, but he was my little man, and I adored him. There is no moment on earth like the moment when you hold new life. None. I will always be so very grateful to God for letting me have those precious moments here on earth.

In fact, I may or may not have held up the Rapture with my 14-year-old prayer begging God to allow me to sit in church holding my baby before I went to heaven. Playing with dolls until I was 10 years old...I named each of them carefully. I dreamed of becoming a mother for quite some time before I held my Chad. He was beyond priceless to me.

Doug seemed to enjoy his son, but never so much that he changed a diaper or opened an eyeball for a night feeding. Little Chad had colic, and it was horrible. I made a joke out of it, saying our night trysts were Chad's way of having special time with his student/mother. Oh, how I loved that little boy, and the whole idea of being a family. Doug seemed to, as well. At one point after a nasty phone conversation with his mom, Doug, with tears in his eyes, lay on our bed with our young son asleep on his chest and said, "I have my own family now." She really hurt him deeply with whatever she said. Berta commonly let her thoughts fly right out of her mouth with no filter, and we had all suffered because of it at one time or another. My heart went out to my husband in his silent sorrow.

Doug was the center of attention and the life of almost any party. He had charisma, but I knew the other side of him…the one that was unsure. Publicly, he would brag about his good looks, athletic abilities, or musical talents to the point of hyperbole; we all would just shake our heads and laugh at how absurd he was. There was merit to his abilities, but I had learned to dismiss his public behavior with a "You're so full of crap" attitude. I was proud to be the wife, the helpmate of this gifted man. I would watch him play baseball and even kept the scorebook. I sat and beamed when he would play his trumpet or guitar on stage. I could see us working together with teenagers…me directing musicals and plays. We just fit. We would always use our skills and talents for Jesus. We would change the world.

I believed, so I poured my life into all the tasks at hand: senior year, my work-study job, little Chad, housework, and writing resumés. Because I worked for the college as a Composition 101 grader, I would come home after classes with a box full of freshman compositions to edit. My job was to note any grammatical or mechanical errors to hand off to the professor for content grading. Since students needed feedback to write their next paper, deadlines were tight. On many nights, I played with Chad by holding toys in my left hand…while grading papers with my right hand. Daddy was working as a security guard at the mall.

When Chad was 9 months old, his parents completed their senior years of college. Doug left school in May with one biology course short of graduation, but with a job lined up as a youth pastor in New Hampshire. I held Chad wearing my graduation cap and gown. I had earned my B.S. degree in English Education and was ready to teach my first set of high school students at age 21.

We packed up the U-Haul with our new Ford Escort in tow and gladly watched our college city and memories fade in the rear-view mirror. It had been such a difficult life there. We were becoming salaried people! The struggle of marriage, going to college, working a part-time job, and keeping our family together was quite a challenge. But that was about to be over; we were grateful to start a new chapter in our lives!

"Can't Live a Day"

recorded by *Avalon*

I Believe

The Apostles Creed

"I believe in God the Father Almighty, Maker of heaven and earth.

And in Jesus Christ, His only Son, our Lord;

Who was conceived by the Holy Spirit, Born of the Virgin Mary;

Suffered under Pontius Pilate; Was crucified, dead and buried;

He descended into Hell. The third day He rose again from
the dead:

He ascended into heaven; And sitteth on the right hand of
God the Father Almighty

From thence He shall come to judge the living and the
dead.

I believe in the Holy Spirit; The Holy Christian Church,
the communion of saints;

The Forgiveness of sins; the Resurrection of the body;

And the life everlasting. Amen."

Chapter Six

We left the Midwest and took our first position as youth pastors on the scenic New England coast. That summer we assimilated to the culture and set up housekeeping in a very old silver trailer until we moved into a two-bedroom Cape Cod style home.

I taught my first year of high school in a Christian academy for a booming salary of $7,000.00. We were happy. I loved teaching and being the wife of a youth pastor.

We had become so creative... establishing social events and Bible and Christian Life studies to show those teenagers how to do life in a relationship with an awesome, omnipresent God. At a lake retreat that year, I created a roadkill menu to feed the group for the weekend. I laughed at myself with that one! Just the cleverness of it all.

Doug directed the Christmas cantata that year: an astounding success with its music, narration, and candlelight for the season. But as beautiful as the cantata was, we had to focus on the clock. Doug and I had to rush out of the sanctuary, drive to the airport, and board our flight to the west. We were headed to be with extended family the next day for Christmas.

Little Chad was having so many important milestones, and I was overwhelmed with joy watching my son grow. At just seven months, he had walked around the coffee table, and by this time, he was truly into everything. Busy, busy, busy! We called him "Big Chad" because he was slight and agile with unending energy! Any sorrow could be displaced by watching him discover the world.

At Easter time, Doug, and I co-directed Dallas Holmes and Praise's, *Rise Again* album as a musical...Doug performed as Jesus, and I was Mary Magdalene. I worked on the costumes, makeup, and sets. We brought the house down with the performance. So great. The youth group was growing.

During one school day, I was called to the office for a phone call; it was my doctor calling to let me know I was pregnant…even while I was on the "mini pill," so you can imagine my shock! But even so, it seemed as though God was smiling on our marriage and our work. I was happy, but that last fall…

I was grading journals from my freshman writing class when I came upon Lise's entry about her love for Pastor Doug and their experience at summer camp. Imagine my surprise! *Did I really just stumble upon this information? Really? I mean she had to know I would read it! Why would she write it?* I had so many questions. This was truly a "hit by a semi-truck" moment. Whatever chapter in Adolescent Psychology class that was in, I had surely missed it. Lise was a scholar in every subject in school. She was lovely, confident, and self-motivated but suffered socially. Teenagers can be so cruel, and Lise's confidence was perceived as arrogance by her peers. She wasn't like them. And though she knew that…she never once attempted to change in order to "fit in," so she was alone. As I read her journal entries about my husband and her feelings for him, I told myself she was confused. Adult attention and kindness would have been so welcomed to Lise; after all, she had been abandoned by both her mother and her father. She lived with her maternal grandmother who attended our church. She sacrificed for Lise so that she could attend private Christian school.

"There had to be a reasonable explanation." Doug was fun and adventurous, but most of all holy. He could be quiet on a dime yet begin singing and playing his guitar…drawing those around him into the presence of God. I thought to myself, I bet she loved seeing him in all those roles. Then, if he had spoken kindly, teased her, or simply taken minutes to listen to her attentively, I could understand her 14-year-old reaction. I was baffled, though, as to why she would write it in her graded school journal knowing that I would not only read it but grade it!

Why would she confess to me? She risked my anger. She risked her grade. I was only 21 years old with a bachelor's degree in English Education; this psychoanalysis was beyond me. I knew I had to talk with, at least, Doug. So, I calmly spoke to Doug about how he needed to be kind, but wise in his future attentions to Lise and read him the entries in her journal. I don't remember any conflict from that conversation. Sick to my stomach about seeing Lise at school, I had simply decided that I wouldn't confront her about the journal but simply return the graded assignment with all the others. After all, I had reached out to the adult in the situation to handle it. Doug was my husband, the father of our soon-to-be **two** children, the pastor/shepherd of this youth group, and my life partner.

He, however, silently responded the next few months by driving her home late at night after several youth group functions. In the last months of my pregnancy, I had not been attending these functions. This happened repeatedly. People were talking, and I confronted him again… begging him to live above the gossip for the sake of our marriage, our children, and our ministry. He insisted he was pure and innocent of the foul thoughts. He said he would not be pressured by people who were determined to read evil into something innocent; to hear him tell it…Doug was a victim of church gossip. I surely knew about church gossips growing up in a minister's home. My parents had been the brunt of so many awful stories, and then, there was my own wretched experience with Berta at the church water fountain when I was 15 with the whole Rock-a-Thon debacle (stupid Doug). *Was that why I believed him? Was he just pushing the right button that would silence me?* The **gaslighting** had begun.

Amanda and Allysa were two new names that had come up as my husband continued his work with our 50-member youth group on the coast of New Hampshire. I heard the whispers at school, the church nursery, and in the foyer on Sundays.

I was embarrassed and ashamed.

Pregnant and powerless.

That's how I felt. I honestly had no idea what to do if I couldn't appeal to my husband to help me. Divorce or separation was not even in the back of my mind. I suppose I could have gone to the senior pastor, but I was so stunned by the behavior and felt safer NOT talking about it to anyone. It just couldn't be real. Looking back now, I am sure I was behaving like a two-year-old who covers her eyes and says, "You can't find me." But I was so very lost; nothing in my life had prepared me for this. My Christian faith and beliefs were solid. God was omnipotent; He had to help me. Christians don't behave this way. My daddy never did this. He always had a policy to keep the door ajar in his office when he was alone with a woman. Either my mom or his secretary would be right outside. I watched my dad protect his integrity all my life. *Why wasn't my husband using this wisdom?*

Then,

I found the video tapes. They were in the underwear drawer. I wasn't trying to find them; I was just putting away clean underwear for my husband. Their pornographic labels gave them away, and the confrontation that ensued resulted in Doug's peaceful explanation he had mistakenly ordered these from some promotional postcard that came to the church office.

I KNOW . . .

When he opened the box in the office with the pastor's wife, he quickly closed it and ran it out to the car to dispose of it in a dumpster later...OR in his underwear drawer!

Yea, I bought that one, too!

Well, Sort of.

No.

[Gaslighting purposely "leads to confusion, loss of confidence . . . uncertainty of one's emotional or mental stability . . ."]

The darkness was swirling all around me. I couldn't see, breath, or think clearly. *HOW did this keep happening?* I loved Jesus. I loved my husband. I loved my children, my job, and our youth group. *What was wrong!?* In a weeping rage, I pulled the black film by the armloads out of its VHS casing declaring forcefully that this THING would not destroy us. Then, I waddled my seven months pregnant self to the trash cans outside and disposed of both tapes!

They survived only for me to find them in the briefcase about nine months later in our new home in Western Pennsylvania.

Oh, Father God,

I could never do tomorrow without the hope you provide. You are my Provider.

LAURIE SULLIVAN

"Precious Lord"

written by Thomas A. Dorsey

I Believe

"He who dwells in the shelter of the Most High will rest in the shadow of the Almighty.

I will say of the Lord, "He is my refuge and my fortress, my God, in whom I trust."

Ps. 91:1-2 (NIV)

Chapter Seven

Two weeks after Brady Douglass was born, we moved to Pennsylvania to pastor a youth group of 150 members. *Were we fired?* I don't know. Doug had lied so much. Looking back, all I remember is Doug looking for a new job sick of the accusations and gossip. The Pennsylvania church flew us out; the church and its administration seemed solid. The youth group had four or five couples in their 40's and 50's who were committed as volunteers, so we would be quite supported in our efforts to lead these teens in a lifetime relationship with Jesus Christ. All I know is I was tired:

pregnant;

mom of an active 18-month-old; and

busy with youth pastor's wife commitments.

I was emotionally beaten down with doubt and lifted in faith to be beaten down again . . .

with the whispers and then the lies from my husband, which always seemed to have a smidge of truth to be somewhat believable and thus the doubt . . . **[Gaslighting purposely "leads to confusion, loss of confidence . . . uncertainty of one's emotional or mental stability . . ."** However, Doug and the senior pastor left it, the church kindly gave us a baby shower that doubled as a goodbye party. So, right before I gave birth, we packed up our home of five and a half months, sold it for a profit of $17,000, but after paying the church back the money they fronted us in the amount of $10,000, we were only left with $7,000. My mom was sick about it. We had such a great job in a beautiful location on the coast. Sitting on the left side of the sanctuary you could see the Atlantic Ocean; she knew how much I adored the sea and was baffled as to why we would ever leave. Daddy had been influential in getting us the job; the senior pastor was his long-time friend, and he knew our integrity...dad's and mine.

Doug always did have "dreams of grandeur," and this new, larger church, along with the three-bedroom split level house we were living in, provided a life that suited him well. Years before at our wedding, Greg, Doug's older brother, had written a poem on a napkin at the reception that confirmed Doug's well-known aspirations:

". . . with his back to the wall

And ready to fall,

Doug will manage to hock something else."

His trumpet, guitars, and his camera had all been hocked through the years as Doug upgraded to the next big thing. So, here we were 600 miles from the sea with those %$##@# video tapes locked in his same briefcase; it would be months before I found them.

While I was busy setting up house, feeding a newborn and caring for now two-year-old Chad, Doug was setting up his spacious and fancy office, directing a youth choir, speaking weekly, and planning a mountain retreat. I got a job as a homebound tutor for the local school district where I would take assignments for teens who were quite sick, suspended, or pregnant under the age of 16. I would work those jobs after Doug got home to be with the boys.

One evening, I returned to the whole upstairs in darkness; the drapes were pulled closed, and all lights were turned off. *What on earth? Where were the boys? Where was Doug? No one should have been sleeping at that time.* I don't remember how he explained that away, but he did, like always.

Panic arrived. Again. But as always, the **gaslighting** was effective; black was white and white was black. Nothing to worry about. Thank God for my boys because if not for them, I truly think I would have shriveled sooner. They gave me strength and such joy.

I found the letter before I found the old porn tapes. Doug had placed his hand- addressed letter to Lise in his official "out" box that was on his mahogany desk to go out on Monday. It was Saturday morning, and he was in rehearsal with the youth choir. When people say, "My heart was in my throat," I now understand. In horror, I just stared daring not to even touch it. *What on earth?*

This was no professional correspondence; it was written by hand in blue ink. Then, I snatched it up and shoved it in my purse with my heart beating so fast. I knew I had to read it and show it to the Pastor and his wife before I ever talked to Doug. He would explain it away in some ridiculous manner where he was innocent manipulating the truth.

Pastor and Jessie read the letter silently while I waited for their response. I remember crying and begging them to help me because Doug would say it was nothing. This was the closest thing I ever had to some sort of objective truth . . . this love letter to an underaged girl of 14. I don't remember the words really, but the hand-drawn sketch of the rocky coast of Maine at York Beach's Nubble Lighthouse is forever in my mind. A guy and a girl were sitting there (at MY ocean) with the caption reading, "our place."

Pastor kept the letter and confronted Doug in front of me and Jesse. There was no wiggling out of it this time, so Doug admitted to an "emotional" affair. *What!? What on earth was an emotional affair!?* Somehow that was supposed to be better than the physical act of intimacy for me and for our pastor. To pastor's credit, he called in the denomination's district authorities and mandated marital counseling. At the time, I didn't wonder why the counseling was not just for Doug. I took guilt upon myself that my husband would need to have an emotional affair. *What was I doing or NOT doing to make him look elsewhere? Affection? Attention?*

Nor did I pursue the fact, that this may have well been a physical affair. Again, nothing in my life had prepared me for this. In the 1980's there was no #Metoo Movement creating a consciousness of the abject normality of men abusing women everywhere and all the time. My husband was a man of the cloth, a minister licensed by a godly denomination. This was before the Catholic church scandals, the fall of Jimmy Swaggert, and many television evangelists. Plus, in my mind, was my righteous dad. Ministers were supposed to be above this. My father would never have allowed suspicion in the first place. If Doug would have followed my father's policies of not being alone with women, we would not be in this mess. Goodness, and my children!!! We had two beautiful, innocent, and precious little boys. They both had their daddy's chocolate eyes. Adventurous Chad and my Elmer Fudd-head, little Brady. Brady had all the chub that Chad had lacked as a baby with his round 'ole bald head and cheeks so big that his lips looked even pouchier. *What about them? We had to fix this marriage at the very least . . . for them. What would little boys do without a dad?*

Oh, heavenly Father . . .

Ode to Loneliness

Whenever I get this feeling,
I have to stop and say, "I love you,"
And remember how far we've come together
You and I.
You are the passion of a lifetime and
The joy of my salvation.
I will desire YOU forever, Lord of mine." (Written in 1985)

I sought refuge where I had always found it…in the presence and care of my Heavenly Father. Since I was four years old, I had always called upon God. *Dear God of my childhood, I am a grown-up now, blinded by pain and baffled with what is and what is supposed to be. Find me here. Help me!*

During that time, we met with our denomination's hierarchy and attended two mandated counseling sessions in Ohio; then I found those two old porn tapes inside Doug's briefcase. I awakened suddenly in the night with the thought I should open the briefcase. I took it downstairs to the laundry room and used a crowbar, and *there they were!* I turned on the dryer to muffle the sound of my guttural cries, feeling lost more than ever. Doug was sick. *How could we go on?*

I longed for the personality test results from our counseling session to give us a clue as to why this was happening. The MMPI-2 test was thorough; I had taken it before to enter the Teacher Education program at my college. The test was a series of 567 statements that could only be answered with a "yes" or a "no." Taking it was enough to make a person crazy if they were not already, but I trusted the test as it had been spot-on about me years ago. I wondered if Doug was a pathological liar. If he were bi-polar. I mean at least then that might explain some of his behavior. I knew his maternal grandmother took medication for schizophrenia, so maybe there was a medical reason he acted the way he did. This seemed important to discover, but I understand now that **gaslighting** occurs for the perpetrator's advantage. Doug, to remain in ministry, needed the cover of his wife and children. And he needed secrecy.

We never found out the results of the test; Doug resigned and moved us to New York telling me he, himself, was a counselor, so he knew what he had to do. He just needed to do it. After only nine months on staff, we would move closer to extended family and our old high school stomping grounds and . . .

be

a

family.

(Oh, how I wanted that.)

Church number three hired him as the youth pastor, and we would begin again!

Turn It Up

"Praise the Lord"

recorded by Russ Taft

I Believe

"As for me, I will continue beholding Your face in righteousness (rightness, justice, and right standing with You); I shall be fully satisfied, when I awake [to find myself] beholding Your form [and having sweet communion with You.]

Ps. 17:15 (AMP)

Chapter Eight

I feel I need to pause and talk about the obvious: "Laurie, what were you thinking? Why did you stay?"

Why do any of us stay? The thousands of us, the millions of us around the world? I wish I had a perfect answer that provided some formula that could be replicated and all women who live with abuse could learn, follow, and become free.

But there is no such formula.

Recently, I have heard a couple of songs that let me know we are not alone. After all, people are writing lyrics and singing songs that mirror what was happening to me. Sara Bereilles wrote and recorded "She Used to be Mine" where the speaker realizes she has lost herself in the experience and is trying to make sense of it all.

When I hear songs like that, I am comforted to know I am not alone and not crazy for being so trusting and wanting to believe in love. Besides, the **gaslighting** was working well. Let's look at that definition again:

1. Psychological manipulation of a person usually over an extended period of time that causes the victim to question the validity of their own thoughts, perception of reality, or memories and typically leads to confusion, loss of confidence and self-esteem, uncertainty of one's emotional of mental stability, and a dependency on the perpetrator

2. The act or practice of grossly misleading someone especially for one's own advantage

(Merriam-Webster dictionary)

I had gotten a job teaching at the Catholic high school in town; they were desperate enough for an English teacher that they hired the Protestant minister's young wife. I was 24-years-old and found a darling young married gal in our church to babysit the boys.

Wow, did I ever learn a lot about Catholicism that year! I am forever grateful for the experience of Ash Wednesday, which will never be the same for me since I witnessed it in school. Our students were given a small piece of paper to write down one sin that beset them, one they struggled with. They filed in towards the priest and the altar where a wok-like pan sat on open flames and dropped their papers in surrendering their struggle to God; the fire of the Holy Spirit would consume the evil. After, the students would gather at the altar again to receive a spot on their foreheads from the ashes made from the pieces of paper; this reminded them of God's power to purify them. To this day, I hold that memory close to my heart...being able to witness this common Catholic ritual through the eyes of my personal relationship with Jesus Christ, in awe of its message and meaning.

That year as my boys grew and Brady developed some light brown traces of hair on his 'ole bald head, I was blessed by my work, our proximity to extended family events, and the "peace" in my marriage. Years later, Max Lucado would write his book, *Just in Case*

You Ever Wonder, which would articulate the well of love in my heart for my precious sons:

"But as you grow and change, some things will stay the same.

I'll always love you.

I'll always hug you.

I'll always be on your side.

And I want you to know that . . . just in case you ever wonder. . ."

Gah, that Max Lucado! Are you crying yet? So, my life went on. I was able to direct a teen musical at church; casting, building the sets, gathering costumes, running rehearsals while my little guys ran around the auditorium brought me so much joy. I have such passion for stories and for teenagers finding their niche wherever it may be, and here, it would be singing or acting. Plus, the whole thing was about Jesus!! Doug directed the singing rehearsals, so we were working together creatively again. The whole church adored our little boys, but no one more than the boys' babysitter,

Elle. She was 17 and extraordinarily vivacious; she reminded me of myself when she acted in the musical and played with our children.

By Easter, I had created an act where I played Mary, the mother of Jesus, at the foot of the cross. As a young mother, myself, I had become increasingly empathetic with how Mary must have felt when she saw her son die. In those moments at the cross, she had to be aware of both roles: he was her son, and he was her redeemer. In full costume, I performed this role ending with the song: "Jesus, Jesus, Lord to Me" by Bill and Gloria Gaither as Mary transitioned from mother to a woman redeemed. The congregation was silenced as I returned to my seat next to Elle to retrieve my wedding ring from her safe keeping: a common theater custom when on stage. The irony of that does not escape me now.

School concluded and Doug decided I deserved a vacation with my side of the family back East after an exhausting year . . . a vacation with my three-year-old and my 10-month-old! Well, I truly would not have had it any other way, so off we flew with Chad on a harness (pre-children Laurie would have been aghast) and

Brady strapped in a baby carrier on the front of me. Turns out, and I wouldn't know for sure until 10 years later, that Doug wanted time alone with Elle. She had come to him for counseling when she and her boyfriend broke up, and somehow, he became her lover: her youth minister, the one she knew she could trust. The one her single mom trusted because, after all, he was a "man of the cloth."

That summer I had food poisoning and subsequently could digest no food for 13 days. Doug frustratedly took me to see a doctor; this task had interrupted his schedule for the day. While waiting to be seen in the waiting area, Doug said, "you should go back to Maine and let your mother take care of you. I'm so busy, but your mom would take care of you and the boys, and you could rest." *What? We didn't even know what was wrong with me yet.*

I felt put off. And though I did not know what was going on, I refused to be shipped back to my mother for the summer. My sickness was treated as irritable bowel syndrome brought on by stress my doctor thought. I think my body knew what my conscious mind did not.

I would suffer from IBS for the next five years until God healed me. So true. I was healed divinely, in a moment of time . . . by my God and Savior! Coolest story. . . tell you in the next book.

In a custody battle 9 years later, I would discover that Elle and Doug were actively having sex while I was gone and were trying to get me to leave again. Isn't it interesting that the physical body can try to express duress when our own mind deceives us. It would still be a while before I would decide to leave.

Doug and I moved into a rental house giving up our apartment after the one-year lease was up. I don't remember why, but it was in that house I had the next confrontations. I found the porn magazines in the basement behind old paint cans, and bluntly asked him what was going on with him and Elle.

One night he went out to buy bottle inserts for Brady's nightly bottle as we used Playtex bottles. Brady never took a pacifier and never sucked his thumb, but he was deeply committed to his nightly bottle! He was crying when we discovered there were no more inserts, so a run to the store a mile away was imperative! Doug left and I rocked and swayed with Brady . . . for TWO hours! Have you ever tried to comfort a screaming child for hours? The longer he cried, the more aggravated I became with Doug. *What on earth? What was taking so long? Should I call the police? Was he in an accident? Was he with Elle?*

Brady finally succumbed to sleep without his bottle. I glared at Doug when he entered the house and futilely demanded to know what took him so long; his BABY needed a bottle! I don't remember anything more of that night. However, I do remember confronting Doug the next morning, as we stood in our living room, overtaken with sunlight…I asked what was going on with him and Elle. He unabashedly stated that he was with her that night in the parking lot of the grocery store "counseling" her; she needed to talk.

I am sure I screamed, "What?" and called it an affair.

"What is wrong with you?" Doug asked, "That girl loves you and these are the filthy things that you think about her!? What kind of Christian are you to think such foul thoughts?"

I was deflated. I didn't know about **gaslighting** back then, but there you have it. A classic case. He knew my buttons: my honest affection for Elle and my faith. Although he got me to shut up, the church was another issue. The rumors were gathering substantially and while everything seemed just slightly off (somewhere in the gray zone), the pastor fired him. Of course, Doug had some lame explanation of how he was victimized, and we went to live in his childhood bedroom...our whole little family.

I insisted we return to counseling and made an appointment with a satellite office of our original counselor in Ohio. We even went, but against his will. When he declared to the counselor, I always brought up the past . . . and that I could never forgive him and move on, the counselor said, "You didn't marry God; you married a woman." I remember it was so soothing to have someone find value in me. Then, of course I beat myself up, checking my heart for unforgiveness toward my husband in case his accusations were true. By then, I had been properly groomed for **gaslighting.**

What I found in those introspective moments, was my own protest. I COULD forgive the past…it's that some things didn't stay in the past. Doug was always up to no good. I forgave the past, but he was evil in the present!

"Held"

recorded by Natalie Grant

I Believe

"When I get really afraid, I come to You in trust."

Ps. 56:3 (MSG)

Chapter Nine

Living in Doug's childhood bedroom was tight. There were two twin beds and a counter that ran the length of one wall with drawers below. The boys slept with each of us or in a sleeping bag on the floor as an adventure. I had just gotten a job as a hostess in a hotel restaurant while Doug would wait for the newspaper to be delivered daily at 2:00 p.m., so he could find a job as well. Doug would drop me off at work by 5:30 a.m. and drop Chad and Brady off to be cared for by Aunt Jo and to play with their cousins. He spent his days alone while I worked. Every afternoon he would come pick me up, stop at Aunt Jo's to gather the boys, and return home. Because we were living with his parents and providing such a pitiful amount of money to care for ourselves, I was conscious of doing household chores at the very least. Good grief, I was hardly making enough to pay our bills and buy diapers for Brady. I remember emptying the China cabinet and dusting every piece in there to help my mother-in-law who not only worked a full-time job but had now become burdened with us. For nearly two months, the routine was the same. I started to panic. *What was the future going to be? We couldn't just live with Doug's parents indefinitely. I should really get a teaching job, but where? Were we staying in this town? Was Doug going to work? He seemed completely content with life as we knew it. What was happening to the man I loved? Was he depressed? How could I encourage him?*

Counseling did not help. We drove to an appointment I made, but the boys were with us because we didn't have a sitter that day. Doug was driving precariously, speeding on the highway. He was swearing at other drivers . . . words I had never heard him say. Words the boys had never heard him say. I snapped because my children were frightened hearing their father. Obviously going to counseling was not what he wanted to do. I prayed. I needed God to show me, to speak to me, to make clear the path. Why? Because Jesus loves me AND us, and only He could and still can help.

What was happening to my marriage dream? We attended church as this "picture-perfect" young family. The façade was beautiful, but didn't God himself believe in a real marriage? *Doug and Laurie were a team . . . for Jesus. We would serve the Lord together. God believes in this, right? And these boys? What about them having a home and a father? What was going on?*

The clarity came around 11:20 p.m. on the day I had worked a double shift. My baby boys were asleep in the bedroom. As I entered the room, I heard the TV playing the movie, Porkies, a stupid R-rated sex movie…WITH MY BABIES IN THE ROOM? Done. I was completely done! I said nothing, felt no more confusion, no more tears or questions. Clarity is one of the most precious things, especially for someone who had been living in a **gaslighting** marriage. The next morning, I called my mom to come get me and the boys. I acted normal and managed to pack up without Doug even knowing. We left; my boys and I were gone! I do not recall the moment we got in the car, what time of day it was, or what car my mom was driving. She and grammie had driven 800 miles, and I just left him.

Never.

Never would his perversion touch them, not while I had breath in my body.

In a new state, I enrolled Chad in my mom's preschool and got two part-time jobs: substituting and teaching adult literacy at night when my parents could watch the boys. I used their car to take little Brady to a babysitter when I substituted. On days I didn't substitute, I spent the noon hour praying at the church. Mom and dad would come home for lunch, allowing me to run over to the sanctuary. Have you ever been in an empty church? It seems so large and so quiet. I chose to lie prostrate in the choir loft and heave-cry to my faithful Heavenly Father! There in the silence of anonymity, in the safest place I knew, in my Father's house, I wept into exhaustion and begged God for mercy. "Please restore my family," I exclaimed! Please help Doug with whatever it is he needs. Please, God, my boys. My boys need their father!"

I was tapped out. I had nothing. I just needed my Savior. Where was hope outside of a supernatural intervention? My mother-in-law called crying, "Please come home, honey. All he does is call your name over and over. Please, honey." Doug had been hospitalized after ingesting a bunch of Tylenol.

"He needs you," my distraught mother-in-law cried, "Please come home, honey."

"He doesn't need me, mom; he needs Jesus," I replied.

How could I explain it all to his mother? Where would I even begin? It was too much, and I didn't even understand it all myself. All I knew was that only Jesus could fix it. Only Jesus.

Doug had mailed us a check for $25.00 to cover expenses "for the boys." Yep, Brady was still in diapers, and we had been there for a month already. After being gone for two months, he flew out to visit us. This after he repeatedly called and begged for another chance. He proclaimed that God had spoken to him, that the boys needed a father, and that he really loved me and was sorry...so, I caved. Those were all the words I wanted to hear, words I had prayed for fervently and continuously to hear. Doug was only in town for a week, and my parents would be right there as a background of sanity for me.

Baby Brady wouldn't look at Doug the whole trip from the airport, after we picked him up; Chad smiled and talked to daddy. Before the week was up, I was pregnant again; he flew home vowing to get a job somewhere (the church would not be the place anymore, eh?). I made no promises as the wounds were still very raw. I vowed to wait and see.

Echoing in my mind was a sentence I still hear from time to time… "You're nobody's fantasy; you are just a regular girl." Yeah, I will wait and see. My Heavenly Father had given me a precious gift through this horror of a marriage, and that gift was from my oldest son."

Chad gave his heart to Jesus in my parents' kitchen while I was washing dishes one night. He was sitting at the kitchen bar looking at a picture of Jesus in his Bible.

"Mommy, the bad men killed Jesus?"

"Um, yes, honey," I answered washing a plate.

"Why, mommy?

I stopped, turned to look at him, and dried my hands; this was a "moment," and the dishes could wait. Have you ever had that experience? I am usually so caught up in completing tasks that sometimes I can miss certain moments. Thank God I didn't miss this!

"Chad, God sent his son, Jesus, to die for us. Our sins, and the bad things we do, would keep us away from God and away from heaven, so Jesus died for us. He loves us and wants us to go to heaven to live with Him someday."

Tears were falling from both eyes of this darling little boy. "Do you want to ask Jesus to forgive your sins and go to heaven with Jesus someday, honey?" He did. It is the honor of my life to have prayed with my firstborn son as he became a Christ-follower at just four-years-old! The faith born in that moment of his life would sustain him through many a storm! What a strong man of God he is today! I am humbled and grateful to have been a part of his redemption story. Chad, my brother in Christ . . . right? God has no grandchildren, and my son here on earth is my eternal brother in the faith! Praise God!

However, in the midst of the joy was the question of Doug. What I knew for sure was limited. Have you ever felt that way?

Jesus loves me. God is good . . . only good . . . always good. I did not want to tell Doug that I was pregnant. I did not want a baby to be the reason he wanted to stay married.

I went to work; I prayed and fasted the noon hour when I wasn't subbing. I treasured my children and waited for God to give me direction. Doug called and said he had gotten a job managing a pizza store in the local mall and had moved into a two-bedroom apartment. In prayer I told God that if Doug was willing to try then I should meet him halfway . . . forgive the past . . . look toward a future with a new baby. *Didn't this baby mean that God believed in our marriage? In our family?* My pastor father received the news of the baby and my intended move pensively, quietly, and prayerfully. He had his own struggle. As a minister he had always taught against divorce, and his own daughter was facing such a monster.

I did not have that same conversation with my mother. She would react with her heart determined to never let her little girl be hurt again. November 20th was the day. My parents drove me six hours south to be picked up by Doug. Doug loaded the three of us into a new, smaller car and drove us home. I was grateful to God for answering my desperate prayers to restore my marriage and family.

On December 3rd, Doug sent me home from the pizza store (he had hired me to run the counter) saying he needed to close. Working there was emotionally difficult. Lots of women came into the store to chat and tease with Doug, obviously knowing him prior to me working there. In those moments, Doug never introduced me as his wife, or publicly declare he was off-limits. It felt off, but I trusted God and steeled my heart against the feelings.

That night he sent me home, I wondered why he had come home so late. He was having sex with Elle. It would be nearly a decade before I found out, but I remember that day distinctly because it was my birthday.

As my pregnancy advanced, I got a job as a homebound tutor for the school district. Chad was in preschool with his cousin. Little Brady was growing and followed his brother everywhere. Those two! Gah, I loved them all up!

"Mommy, we made fire," they said one Saturday morning. I made the misguided parent decision to assume the quiet of that Saturday morning . . . quiet after 7:00 a.m. meant they were sleeping in. Nope. Though I was eight and a half months pregnant sleeping in a waterbed, I moved at the sound of their voices. My two-year-old and four-year-old said, "Mommy, we made fire." They surely did. It was perfect. Just like they saw daddy's the night before. To their credit, the fire was in the fireplace. They had positioned the sticks into an excellent teepee and crumpled newspaper into balls underneath that. If I wasn't so terrified . . .and if they weren't so YOUNG, I would have patted them on the back, celebrating their skills. Instead, I said, "Oh, honey!!!! Only daddy makes the fires!" I don't remember what Doug did or said but he handled it.

Family life was in full swing, but I was still married by myself. I just didn't see it.

"Can You Reach My Friend?"

recorded by Debby Boone

I Believe

"My life is well and whole, secure in the middle of danger…"

Ps. 55:18 (MSG)

Chapter Ten

Life went on as we waited to meet our new bundle of joy. I liked tutoring because I could be with my boys more often as opposed to the hours at the pizza restaurant. Living by extended family was so joyful as the boys could play with their cousins. We also got to attend our home church with family! One Sunday night I chose to go to church even though the guys were staying home. When I returned, I saw Doug masturbating in the walk-in closet with some magazines and baby oil.

Exhausted with grief, I broke before God and Doug. *How could this be? Where was God?* All I had done was walk into the door of my bedroom, notice a light in the closet, observe my husband, fall onto the bed and weep.

I had nothing. Nothing. All the prayer. All the fasting.

I truly do not remember what Doug said because, as usual, he talked God words. Hollow God words. Spinning language as only one who **gaslights** another human can do.

I was spent. Crying wasn't a luxury I could afford for any length of time because the boys were sleeping in the room next to ours. My pillow would stay stained with tears for several more years as I waited for a miracle from my faithful God. It seemed a small town that was two and a half hours away would be the miracle. Doug announced he had been hired to pastor this tiny congregation and that the district superintendent of the denomination's state office had told him this was his "last chance, so don't blow it."

Josh was born that June, a gift to my soul, the nine pounds chubby one! Looking at his innocence and the new love in the eyes of his older brothers who wanted to "hold the baby" ensured me our miracle was on its way. He was only one-month-old when we passed by the sign that read "Canbury - 12 miles" on our way to a new little church where we would begin yet again! Our sweet little family of four was now five! Oh, how I hoped the words Doug said about giving up the porn and living for God were true. This was our last chance.

In our first year, a congregation of 12 nearly grew to a hundred! We worked so hard! Doug led worship and preached charismatically; he started a youth group on Wednesday nights while I taught adult Bible study upstairs. Our boys were loved on in the church nursery while we ministered. People came from other congregations to witness the dynamic worship, and the young minister and his little family! We certainly looked the part of a godly clan and so young; we were in our twenties. The boys were six, four, and one…all with their daddy's chocolate brown eyes.

Doug had me dress them up for our Mother's Day luncheon held in the basement of the church. He surprised every woman there by gathering the boys and singing Bette Midler's *"Wind Beneath My Wings,"* in which he professed via song that I was his hero, and the "wind beneath [his] wings." Honestly, it was stunning, and I so very much wished it was real. As our ministry grew in that first year, I babysat two boys to bring in money while I stayed home with our three sons and lived on food stamps.

"We won't need assistance for long," I explained cheerfully as I signed my name on the form for the food stamps. "Our congregation is just so small right now." One year later we were no longer on food stamps. Oh, how good God was to us as we threw ourselves wholeheartedly to growing a solid faith in Christ for the people He sent to us! So many positive things were happening; one of our board members sold us a used car he had inherited and didn't need. Now, I had a vehicle to run to the grocery store and take the boys to the park where they could run and play! Oddly, though, Doug had purchased a wooden sailboat from someone, parked it in our garage, and said he was going to refurnish it. Yikes! I was torn about that financial decision; however, I remembered that my own father, a minister, worked for a couple of years building a kit car with a Volkswagen chassis in his garage. I swallowed my fear about spending money we didn't have on such a useless item when we had three growing boys and reasoned that, perhaps, there were stresses in ministry that I did not understand; thus, Doug needed a project.

"Laurie, there is a teaching job advertised in the paper!" Patricia exclaimed on the phone. "I thought of you right away because it's an English job." And that, dear readers, is how God provided me a job in my profession mid-school year when I wasn't even looking for one. Goodness, I would have to apply, do an interview, hope my brain hadn't turned to mush since it had been three years since I last taught. My mind was consumed with pop culture and Bible stories for boys under the age of six. *What are teenagers even thinking these days?* When the interview was over, I yelled, "I've still got it," as I danced around my kitchen!

God also provided the most nurturing woman to provide care for four-year-old Brady and 18-month-old Josh. All working moms know how desperately important it is to have peace knowing that your little ones are not only safe, but also loved while you work. Now, we had money to do things like take a vacation! That spring we took the boys to the coast, and the church broke ground on the addition to our little two-bedroom parsonage, which would provide a living room, master bedroom and bath.

Every Saturday morning at 7:00 a.m., volunteers arrived to spend the day on construction. I was up with doughnuts and coffee for the workers. Women arrived at lunchtime with food, and our boys loved all the glorious activities! I began to see signs of Doug's former self more and more. I did not want to see them; I wanted the work we did for Jesus to be pure. I wanted our boys to have two parents, to grow up like I did safe and happy knowing the love of family and Christ! But disaster was on its way whether I chose to see it or not, and a decade later I would discover that Elle and Doug had been writing to each other the entire time. His letters were dreadfully pornographic, she said, and when the relationship ended, Elle's mother insisted on keeping those letters in a box in their attic as evidence. "Evidence," she said for the day this sordid affair would be blamed on her daughter by the church." Elle offered me the box that year we talked. I declined but kept the knowledge it existed in case I needed some objective, nasty proof I lived some stupid parallel life with a man hiding behind the cloth.

Turn It Up

"Because He Lives"
recorded by Bill and Gloria Gaither

I Believe

"The Lord is my rock, my fortress and my delivers; my God is my rock, in whom I take refuge, my shield and the horn of my salvation. He is my stronghold, my refuge and my savior—from violent men you save me. I call to the Lord, who is worthy of praise, and I am saved from my enemies."
2 Samuel 22: 2-3 (NIV)

"God is bedrock under my feet, the castle in which I live, my rescuing knight. My God—the high crag where I run for dear life, hiding behind the boulders, safe in the granite hideout; my mountaintop refuge, he saves me from ruthless men."
2 Samuel 22:2-3 (AMP)

Chapter Eleven

The good news? God had already provided two things I didn't know I would certainly need for my future: a car and a job. In my second year of teaching, I joyfully accepted the offer to direct a community musical in the little neighboring town where I taught. What a gift to my heart it was to be involved in theater again! My dear older colleague was the music director, and we auditioned a cast for *South Pacific* to be performed in the Spring. Another blessing was that Chad and Brady could attend school with me as a benefit of the job. We were together in a K-12 building in an adorable farming town that reminded me of Mayberry RFD and the Andy Griffin Show.

The church was still growing, I believe because of our Sunday night bonfires that lasted through the summer into late Fall. As a congregation, we would meet at the church at 6:00 p.m. and conduct a service that lasted about an hour and would reconvene in the backyard of the newly finished parsonage. We would roast hot dogs and marshmallows and listen to Doug and a couple of other guys strum worship music on their guitars as the children ran around freely, and the women sat in lawn chairs. We felt like an enormous family; my heart was full. I had also started teaching a high school Sunday School class, and we hired a part-time youth pastor who had a fantastic wife! That freed Doug to teach on Wednesday evenings while Trent and Jessie taught the youth.

Ugly arrived clearly one night in mid-May. I returned home from *South Pacific's* dress rehearsal that literally lasted until midnight. It was crunch time for production. The musical added the necessary technical aspects of light and sound in the school gymnasium that was transformed for six theater performances. I was bone tired as the many hats I was wearing seemed to be stacked on top of my head all at the same time; the pressure was on to grade all the papers piled inside my briefcase, parent, and fulfill church obligations and commitments.

I walked in the back door, through the kitchen and living room, and into my silent sleeping house, thankful for the waiting comfort of my bed. I didn't see the blanket and pillow at first on the couch. It wasn't until I tried to turn the doorknob to our bedroom door that I stopped and glanced around. I tried the door again. Oh, it was definitely locked! I was locked out of the entire master bedroom suite. *What is going on, I wondered?* Nothing like this had ever happened before. Because I was exhausted, I simply returned to the living room and slept on the couch, in my clothes until the next morning when I could gather some thought.

While I do not remember our exact conversation, how I handled getting dressed the next morning, or how I got the children fed and ready for school and off to Miss Lily's house, I do remember the anger in Doug's voice. He accused me of having an affair while I worked under the pretense of "directing a musical." Dumbfounded. That's the word! I was absolutely dumbfounded; this was completely absurd.

First of all, me?

Secondly, me?

Thirdly, I

am

exhausted!

Ain't nobody got time or energy for such evil doins'!

There was not one thing to do to fix the situation, so while the clock was ticking, I put one foot in front of the other and went to work (which, by the way, was followed by another dress rehearsal and three subsequent performances that weekend).

The technique of manipulation here, is called **projection.** This is when a person places his/her own unacceptable choices onto another person. Looking back, I realize my directing that musical in a neighboring town upset Doug's control over me. I had entered successfully into a world where he knew no one and had no influence. It must have shaken him. Meanwhile, I was singing to God on the way to work and all the way home! So grateful to be alive outside of the fog, the gray that had permeated my life for over seven years. Doug did attend one of the performances and interacted with scores of people who said they loved me and the joy I had given the community in this production! No more was ever said about an "affair," and church activities peeked with Vacation Bible School and the return of Doug's brainchild, Friday in the Park, downtown in the gazebo.

He had started bringing his guitar and church sound system to the center of downtown the summer before. Some of the guys joined him on guitar and several gals from the worship team would take turns if it fit their summer vacation schedules. It had really been a bold move in a town where Christianity was not a celebrated thing. The fact Doug had been written about in the local paper for actively speaking out against pornography in the small community only furthered his public presence; people came to see this guy. A couple of Fridays into the park event, Doug told me to drive our boys home so they could go to bed; he would return the equipment to the church and get a ride home. This tired mama agreed and went to sleep herself before he got home. He wasn't home the first time I got up to go to the bathroom, but I didn't think anything of it. The next Friday when I was pulling away with the boys in the van, I saw he was getting in the car with one of my high school Sunday School gals, Angela. That was odd; surely, he was going to help the guys pack the equipment.

And, ugh! Getting in the car with a 17-year-old blonde? Not this again. We had lived through all this conversation before . . . about the "appearance of evil" about how no minister, teacher, counselor, etc. should put himself in a compromising position. Preserve his reputation. Live above reproach. Don't give people something to talk about.

And, good grief, what about me? *What does that action do to me? Did he want to send me reeling back into the horrific past where the rumors and the "emotional affairs" nearly did me in?* Memories of Lise, Amanda, Allysa, and Elle ran across my mind. *Did I, Laurie, have to remind him of this again?* Argh!

Or worse. Was it happening again?

Angela was a vivacious teenaged girl who started coming to the church one summer because of the Friday nights downtown. Her family didn't attend, but she drove herself to church; I admired this girl. My own mother had a story of how she found out about Jesus at a summer tent service when she was 16. Mom's five brothers would make fun of her. Angela was brave, I thought, and fun to talk to! She was in my high school Sunday School class, so it was my privilege to talk with her about Jesus.

It was too much . . . the more I thought about it. So very dejá vu. Elle was 17. She was vivacious. I really liked her . . . felt a connection with her . . . had her babysit my boys. I shook my head almost to force the thoughts to fall out. *It couldn't be. I wouldn't live through it this time. I wouldn't make it.*

There was talk . . . the whispers and the sideways looks. I confronted Doug in his church office . . . loudly. No one was there.

"WHAT is going on with you and Angela?"

"Nothing. What are you talking about?

DON'T lie to me. Do not LIE to me!" I shouted firmly as I slapped him good and hard across the face. Trembling, weeping, and in shock at what I had just done, I walked out of the office and drove home. What was happening to me? Who was I? What would happen to my whole world now?

Doug reacted differently than he had before. He reassured me over and over there was nothing happening, saying all the words people say when they want you to believe them only in a more compassionate tone. He added that several men from the church were always there packing up, too, and that he would not be doing anything stupid in front of them.

For whatever stupid reason, I believed him . . . maybe because I was so shocked at my own violent reaction; I don't know.

In August, we drove north to visit my parents for two weeks . . . well, the boys and I stayed a full two weeks.

Doug and Lily's husband, Tony, had planned to drive through the night to drop me off at my grandmother's house, five hours from my family. After unloading me and the three boys, they would turn around and drive 13 hours back home. Since Tony and Lily had once lived in the northern town where my parents were, they were excited to spend a week there with us when Doug and Tony's family (Lily and their two teenaged sons) would drive north the following week to "pick us up." Tony was a member of our church board and Lily had been our daycare provider for Josh since he was 18-months-old. They were a darling couple with boys about seven years ahead in development from our own sons. We watched and learned how to raise some good boys (and learned how much teenage boys could eat!). For a couple of years now we had exchanged memories of living in the northern part of America, so this trip was all the unicorns and cupcakes it could ever be. Except. . .

Except that Doug and Angela were seen going into the parsonage.

Except that Tony himself had unknowingly stumbled upon them entering the sanctuary to vacuum; they were sitting on the steps of the altar. Doug with his guitar singing to Angela. Tony didn't tell me about that when we joyfully frolicked on vacation with his family for a solid week and then made an 18-hour journey home. Tony told me after we had been fired. He told me nearly a year later after I had written the letter to Doug, telling him to leave. *Why, Tony? Why did you not tell me?*

Within a week of returning home, Doug had several board meetings. I was consumed with getting the boys ready for a new school year and prepping my classroom for a new year. That and the laundry . . . so much laundry all the time, especially after a two-week vacation. Finally, Doug got me alone and told me we had been fired; he had found us a rental as Denny, a church member in his mid-twenties, had inherited a house he didn't live in.

"What happened? Why? What is going on?" were my natural questions as my gut twisted in the familiar agony of discovering that my life was not really real . . . the part I lived in just ran parallel to the real life that moved along without my knowledge.

"I'm calling Jason and Drew!" I gasped, thinking these two godly men, these board members would provide the sanity I needed in understanding this horror.

"No, you're not. You think they LIKE you, Laurie? They don't. They hate you," he replied.

"What?"

"It's true. You do not understand people at all. They called me in earlier this week mad about the fact that I left the lights on in the church for days when we left town. Then they went and interviewed the guy who was preaching for us in our absence. This is all just an excuse to get a new guy to pastor. I never want to talk to any of them again."

Gaslighting.

My shock and panic took second place to the fervor of activity that took place in the next few weeks. I had to remain calm and full of joy for the sake of Chad who was now eight, Brady who was six, and Josh who was three. Chad and Brady had birthdays 11 days apart; we packed a three-bedroom house and started a new school year while Doug decided he would open a counseling practice in the city 40 minutes away.

Here we were facing the loss of our home, income, support group, our extended Christian family, bonfires, etc., but there was no time to grieve… just move on… keep moving….

Why did I just do life at status quo? I don't know. At first, it was probably survival since the bottom of the world had just dropped out from below my feet. Then, I do know that my children needed me to be steady so they would not be frightened by the drastic changes. Their school would be the same, but the church they attended with their friends more than three times a week was suddenly gone. At least Lily was still willing to babysit Josh, but we never talked about the church or what happened. Tony and Lily stored much of our furniture in their basement since Denny's rental house was fully furnished. After living in a foggy stupor, I was jolted to reality when the school counselor called my classroom:

"Laurie, Chad is hysterical. Come as soon as you can."

"Where Could I Go?"

recorded by the *Gaither Vocal Band*

I Believe

"For in Him we live and move and have our being."

Acts 17:28

Chapter Twelve

Second grade Chad would be formerly diagnosed with "school phobia." For real. I had no idea that was a thing. He started his panic cries at 5:30 a.m., waking me up to tell me he didn't want to go to school. It was dreadful. My little guy.

After speaking with my superintendent, he said to me, "Laurie, let him stay home. Tell him he can stay home until his heart is ready to go to school."

"What? What if his heart is never ready to go? Couldn't this backfire?"

"I think he will be ready."

"Okay," I said and prepped Chad to go to the babysitter with little Josh.

We told Chad he could tell us when his heart was ready. I suppose this technique was one to relieve the pressure and give Chad some ownership or power over his own life. He didn't go to school for a whole week as I battled to figure out how we got here and how we would ever return to any kind of normalcy.

We lived in Denny's rental house from September until February when Chad's school phobia started. We lived six months in some strange and uncertain limbo; in a house where the furniture was not even familiar…except for the boys' bunkbeds we put in their room. We felt they should be together after so much upheaval. This would be the 12th home Chad had lived in throughout his eight years of life. For pity's sake, no wonder he was paralyzed with anxiety!

Going to work each day with only Brady, I had my own anxiety. Here I was a public-school teacher whose child was not able to attend school; as his mother, I had no solutions, so I went where I had always gone . . . to Jesus.

What do I do, Lord? Help your girl!

And I waited. I waited for so many things to be resolved. Things only divinity could solve. Everything was beyond me. The marriage, our living situation, our lack of a support system, our church family, money, and now Chad.

Doug convinced me to get my father to co-sign on a loan from my school credit union so he could open an office in the city. Yep, my father. My father who clearly told all three of his children he would never co-sign a loan. This guy was a worker, and he believed in everyone working for what they got in life. He was the son of a potato farmer in northern Maine and was one of 13 children. In September, school would let out for two weeks in Aroostook County, so all the children could harvest potatoes and earn their own money for clothes and school supplies. My sister tried picking one year when she lived there during high school. Mom said she came home and lied on the couch in her clothes…not moving for 12 hours! Haha! So glad I never tried. Yikes. But this explains my dad. My dad who believed in work.

"Dad," I cried, "We really need a loan from my credit union, so Doug can work! We have no income except my teaching. I know you said you would never co-sign, but you know it would be paid back because it will be a payroll deduction, and we need money, dad. Please think about it."

"I will," he responded miraculously.

Daddy signed the papers.

We made business cards. Doug rented a space and began to advertise. He chose to work at night since so many people worked during the day and needed evening appointments. We saw him only on the weekend, and every month my paycheck paid down the loan. We had enough money coming in, so I didn't question Doug's employment; however, I don't remember how much he generated. I do know when I told him to leave the house, he spent a month "working" to save enough money to leave me.

So, that's how we lived. I waited for God to guide me through this foggy limbo of life... where my child was suffering, and I was robotically putting one foot in front of the other. Church life was bizarre. Doug's brother, Greg, had moved out of state to pastor another congregation leaving behind a precious growing group of believers in a neighboring town. Greg convinced the church board to hire Doug as an interim pastor while they searched for his replacement. Every Sunday our little family of five drove 45 minutes to church and ate out because the boys were starving facing a 45-minute ride home.

"Where do we want to go today?" Doug would ask cheerfully.

"Burger King!

"Pizza Hut!"

"Wendy's!" the boys would chorus, oftentimes arguing about who had chosen the place the last time. Our lives had lost the coveted family feeling of a homemade Sunday dinner around the table, creating memories with my guys.

After nearly two weeks, we finally insisted Chad return to school. I told him that mommy was there at school if he needed her, and that he could leave his classroom to go talk with the counselor or school psychologist when he needed to. Plus, he had scheduled visits weekly with the psychologist, so we felt as though we were providing some good scaffolding for his anxiety. Did it ever dawn on me that his anxiety was due to the upset in our home? Yes.

That is why Doug and I tried not to argue in front of the children. Could Chad sense my frustration and disappointment? I am sure he did; he was and still is a sensitive soul. Often, Doug's actions caught me off guard when I would find him passed out on the living room couch with multiple Benadryl pills popped out of the aluminum foils.

Who does that?

Why?

For heaven sakes, what is going on? The boys only get to see him on Saturday and Sunday . . . he isn't even sick.

By March I was aware that change was imperative. When Doug came downstairs with a pack of Marlboros showing through his dress shirt pocket, I had to face the fact he was not the man of God I had married, and things were getting desperate. I used to sit in the congregation listening to him preach adoringly. What conviction! A man of honor.

"I wish I could come home with the man in the pulpit," I had said one Sunday afternoon.

"You do," Doug nonchalantly replied.

"I don't, though," I sighed, and that was it.

Life was a new kind of terrible. I resigned from the worship team at church when I spotted Mackenzie Jones in the congregation. I saw her without her husband, Jackson and witnessed her face as she gazed at Doug. What was Makenzie doing at this church 45-minutes from home? She and Jackson attended our former church. Doug told me she was coming to him in the city for marriage counseling, but my gut hit the floor when reality dawned.

Once again. My parallel life was being revealed. Doug who had confessed to several "emotional affairs" with young girls in our youth groups. Doug who confessed only when he was caught by some objective evidence or a senior pastor. What a fool I had been. The only reason Mackenzie would be here without Jackson was foul play, but I still did not know

what

to

do.

I confronted Doug, but, really, what was the use? It always produced the **gaslighting** and projection techniques.

"Doug, I cannot prove anything, but I KNOW that this is wrong. Whatever is going on I will not be a part of it. From now on, I will sit at the back of the church with the children. I will not say anything to anyone, but you better pray that no one asks me why I am no longer singing with you because I WILL tell them if they ask."

Dear God, help me. Help me. Help me.

There was no way I wanted to be divorced. God himself says in Malachi, "I hate divorce." I did not want to lose my Doug, but, I had already lost him.

I wanted to be married, to grow old with a man I adored, but I only adored him as the preacher in the pulpit who was charismatic and holy.

I wanted to parent my darling boys with their father, the one who was there the day they were born.

I wanted to share financial responsibilities and decisions about our future. I wanted a partner. Someone who could be strong when I wasn't. Someone who could make me be a better version of me and help bring out the best in me. And someone I could be a blessing to.

I wrote a prayer for Doug in those months and read it to his minister brother, Greg, on the phone. "Those are beautiful words, Laur (his nickname for me). They need to be read someday to someone who deserves them," he replied.

Sigh. I just waited for direction from my Savior…the One who knows me best and loves me the most.

"In Christ Alone"

recorded by Michael English

I Believe

"The prayer of a righteous man is powerful and effective."

James 5:16 (NIV)

Chapter Thirteen

My answer came that Friday night in March as I was washing dishes. James Dobson's book, *Love Must Be Tough* that I bought at our local bookstore, proposed something I had never heard in Evangelical circles: Christian separation. I am sure as a reader living in the #MeToo world, you might be screaming by now: "Get out! Report him!" But this was the 1980's and no one spoke of these things, especially not in the government, and certainly not in the church. The late 80's did, however, bring some drama.

Marvin Gorman's sex scandal of 1986 (Doug and I knew him personally. He was once a speaker in our church)

Jim and Tammy Faye Bakker's scandal (1987)

Jimmy Swaggert's famous, "I was wrong" sex scandal of 1988.

I remember the day I heard about Jimmy Swaggert's prostitute; I grabbed my Bible holding it close to my chest and wept bitterly. If the man of God has gone to hell, what hope is there for the rest of us? Except. Except that God was not responsible. Jimmy was. Except I would not choose Jimmy's path. I hated infidelity. Hated it with every bone in my body.

Even though these examples of sin in high places were made public, it was still not a world where the average pastor's wife had any resources. Who does she talk to? Who can she tell that she suspects her husband of having affairs? That he looks at porn? That he masturbates? Are you kidding me? No one. Not a single soul.

Professional marriage counseling would be the only safe place to talk. But chances are both spouses needed to attend the counseling . . . Doug would not go.

"I am a professional counselor, Laurie. I know exactly what to do. I just don't do it," Doug exclaimed.

With that, the only thing I had left to do was follow Dobson's theory of Christian separation where I would draw a line of boundary that said, "I will not continue like this." And you know the rest.

There is much to be said for peace in a home, and that is what we had, me and my sons. We focused on us; God sent Grampy and Nana for a visit in April as they traveled south; they visited again in May when they headed back home. School was in full force for this New York state high school teacher with preparation for, and grading Regent Exams. And then the end-of-year evaluation with the principal that would send life in a new direction.

"Sign here, Laurie, stating that you realize that this is year two of employment, and you have three years to acquire the needed master's degree or lose your job," Mr. Richards explained.

"Tom, I know. What I don't know is what to do. You know I am newly separated from Doug. My checks end in June; I live in a rental house that I will not be able to pay for..."

"I have an idea," he said. Goddard College in Vermont. They offer a progressive program of study where you live on campus the first week of the semester, write your semester plan with your advisor, and then go home to work mailing in your papers every three weeks."

What? I am sure I cried as one of my many heavy burdens had just been lifted. I let out a sigh of relief. There was hope. Hope I would not lose my job. May and June were crammed with end-of-school field trips and activities for the boys, and the longest application known to mankind for me to apply to grad school. Mom and Grammie came to the rescue and lived with us in June because we needed to pack up the house amongst many other things. My paycheck was ending. We headed north for the summer with an uncertain future ahead of me. All I knew was...

- God is faithful, and He is good.

- I will have a job in September.

- My boys are safe.

- I was headed to grad school.

Meanwhile horrid things continued to occur in the Doug arena.

- He broke into the house and took the 25-inch television, leaving a 13-channel black and white 13-inch in its place. We were at church.

- He called on Mother's Day. I was ironing all our church clothes. He told me we should go to church together as a family. It would be good for the children.

That sounded like it would be good for the boys . . . sitting in God's house with their parents. He knew that would make me think because he always knew what was important to me, what I wanted for our lives and for our children . . .

"No, Doug."

"No, I will not do that. It is a lie," I mustered with all the strength within me. He talked some more mocking me, criticizing me, **gaslighting** as usual. I said a firm goodbye, hung up, and fell over the ironing board crying out to God. Such a cool thing happened next.

It was 8:30 a.m. on a Sunday morning and the radio played *Revialtime* as it always did. Rev. Dan Betzer was speaking from Acts chapter five about Ananias and Sapphira. Any kid raised in Sunday School would know that both ended up dead on the floor of the sanctuary for lying to the Holy Spirit. *Who lies to the Holy Spirit anyway? Plus, to lie to Him IN the church?* Any kid had the fear of God knocked into them way back in time. There would be no lying in the church or anywhere else. However, that day, Pastor Betzer pointed out something I had never seen before about this familiar story. Sapphira could have been spared.

She didn't have to die with her husband. He suggested a different path where Sapphira would draw a line for righteousness in her own life, where she would say an emphatic NO. No, I will not participate in this lie with you, my husband. Betzer proposed at the very least she could have saved her own life and at the most could have persuaded Ananias to change his mind.

But she did not draw that line.

Sapphira died. At the altar. In church.

I wept while I ironed my dress and three little shirts. I wept for the kindness of Divinity. Of a God that saw my tortured heart, torn between what I knew was right and my own doubt that I was not right.

No, Doug, I will not participate in that lie with you that we are a happy Christian family celebrating Mother's Day. You don't even live here. You are sleeping with whatever. You don't support us. You are not a husband. For a person who has been **gaslighted** for nearly a decade such clarity was a most precious, precious thing.

The private investigator followed him for a week (a professional who owed a favor to one of my friends) and reported back: "You NEED to divorce him!" "Why, though?" I asked wanting so desperately to understand what was in the fog that I had lived in? What was happening in the parallel life that I didn't know or have any evidence of?

"The women are of every size and color going in and out of the motel room. Now, they could say they are playing checkers in there, but I doubt it," the P.I. firmly reported.

Since it was the age of the HIV era, and the world was aware this was a sexually transmitted disease along with needle transmissions, I was jolted into a clear reality. This investigator whom I did not know had no reason to lie to me, and I knew I would have to pursue divorce.

Doug tried to use my name, Social Security number, work record and credit history to buy a used BMW in a neighboring town. The school secretary had called me out of class for an urgent call in the office from the dealership; the employee told me he was suspicious when Doug came by himself to the car lot, took the application, and returned the next day with it filled out and signed, yet he had never actually seen me.

So now, it was my limited finances in jeopardy. What if that dealership had not called me? That would be yet another loan I would be paying. The loan that daddy had signed for would not be paid off for another two years. Doug knew that. He never once offered to pay his debt. Again, I realized I needed to pursue divorce.

So, in the fervor of field trips, nightly homework, Regents exams, averaging grades, writing local exams, holding review sessions, applying for grad school, packing my rental house, etc., I made an appointment to see a lawyer. I had never met a lawyer. I hadn't even seen Judge Judy on television, but daddy had loved Perry Mason episodes, so that's all I had to go on.

He seemed like a typical lawyer with the large private office lined with important looking books; he was even seated behind a large cherry wood desk, listening to me as I told my story. When I concluded, he leaned forward across that expanse and said, "Divorce from a minister. What does THAT do to your faith?" and for the first time in a long time, I spoke promptly with resolve:

"Doug didn't give me my faith; he cannot take it away!"

I sat back in the chair thinking, "Wow, that was good!" and thanking the Holy Spirit of God himself for that realization. I'm usually not that quick at the draw!

Because Doug would not sign the divorce papers, we would leave town once school was finished without being divorced. Mom and Grammie loaded up their car with some of our stuff. I borrowed a car rack from my new pastor to load the boys' bikes, roller blades, skateboards, basketballs, and such on the top of the car. I stuffed textbooks for grad school in there as well.

The two cars pulled out of town. One boy was riding in style all alone in Mom and Grammie's backseat not having to share anything with any brother! I was driving with one son in the front seat, a known place of privilege for a child, and one occupying the backseat not having to share a thing, either. It was going to be a glorious 18-hour trip! In the rearview mirror was life as I knew it, as we all knew it. What was ahead was mostly unknown. We would live with no money in my parents' home; I even needed to ask for $500 for grad school. Somehow, we would come back in three months to my job and their school, but where would we live?

Doug told me he would pay $50 a month for child support and "that was more than any court could make him pay." Would he? Not much about my life was real;

he had lied about everything. I could feel the waves of nausea flooding my body as I passed through the last of our town and onto the county road. Oh, no! No . . .

I flashed my lights and beeped my horn a couple of times to signal Mom ahead of me to stop. I ran from my car to the side of the road and vomited all the way to the dry heaves. My mom took over as the driver of my car while my grammie drove the other car. I became a passenger in the front seat as I closed my eyes and slept safely in the arms of my God, and the loving care of my family...until another day when God would save me again, and again, and forever.

Epilogue

It's a hot July summer day in 2022, 30 years after the pain. I am letting tears run down my face as I listen to a song my Brady sent via text directing me to YouTube: "Talking to Jesus." I hit play again and again. Gah! Beeps from the family text feed keep interrupting with pictures of my Chad and his Laura celebrating 15 years of marriage. What a faithful God!

"I'll be talking to Jesus. . . for the rest of my life." Beep. Josh and his Victoria in a cute vacation shot on the water. Just the two of them without their precious little boy and girl. What a faithful God!

"He'll be talking to Jesus . . . for all of his life." Beep. Brady answers a tech question for me from 800 miles away as he sits with his family: Emma, his bella verde, and darling boy. What a faithful God!

I find Zach Williams and Dolly Parton's, "There Was Jesus" on my Spotify and play it loudly, standing in the center of my bedroom floor arms open wide and face turned to the sky, to the forever faithful God who sees. . . and knows. . . and lives within me and through me. And I, Laurie Jean . . . am speechless.

Strategies

When disaster strikes here are some suggestions for your mental and spiritual health.

✓ **Turn it up!**

Create a playlist of doctrinally sound God music! Turn it UP!

✓ **Read aloud! The Mae Method**

My mother, Mae, taught me, as a teenager to use the Bible in this unique way. Read it out loud when Satan shows up with his rotten lies, so she would say aloud, "O.K. Satan, if you are not going to leave me alone, I am going to read to you."

Then, she just opened the Bible and started reading from wherever she opened it to! It could have been the heave offerings of Leviticus; she didn't care. It was truth. It was God's word, and it had power.

✓ **Write the TRUTH** on index cards/sticky notes. Girls, post them EVERYWHERE (even on your steering wheel, eh?)

Resources

In 2022, a Google search produced many resources when I typed "resources for counseling ministers' wives."

www.smallchurchministry.com

1-844-727-8671 (1-844-PASTOR) 8 a.m. – 10 p.m. EST

www.careforpastors.org The Ephesians House (They even have a Facebook group)

www.biblicalcounseling.com Counseling Wives of Men in Ministry

www.leighpowers.com There are online communities!

www.alongsideministrywives.com So many resources.

https://www.gracelifeinternational.com

And it turns out that individual church denominations now offer retreat spaces and counseling services to the pastor, the wife, and the children!

About The Author

Laurie Sullivan is an accomplished teacher, writer, and speaker. Raised in a loving home, her mother and father were ordained ministers. She graduated from high school a year early, obtained her B.S. in English Education and later a M.A. and Ed. Specialist degree. She holds teaching certifications in Missouri, New York, and Maine. Throughout her career she earned the SMIC Teaching Fellowship 2019 in Shanghai, China, and published in the EARCOS Journal Spring 2020 her article "Enjoying

Classroom management, really!" In the Midwest she was named the Missouri State Teachers Association Southwest Secondary Educator of the Year in 2017 and Unsung Hero in 2018; served as President of MSTA in Springfield, Missouri; and served as Ozarks Writing Project Teacher Consultant through Missouri State University. In 2008 she published her children's book, Noise in the Night, with her oldest son as illustrator. She is the mother of four sons, an adopted daughter and three stepdaughters and nana to thirteen! Laurie enjoys her precious family, viewing, acting, and directing theater, the ocean, and traveling. She is a vibrant public speaker bringing a message of encouragement and hope to beleaguered women. She and her husband, Rob, live in Lubec, Maine. To connect her visit her website at www.victoriousanyway.co